D1520977

CHASING
A TORNADO

BY MARK HARASYMIW

Gareth Stevens
Publishing

Please visit our website, www.garethstevens.com. For a free color catalog of all our high-quality books, call toll free 1-800-542-2595 or fax 1-877-542-2596.

Library of Congress Cataloging-in-Publication Data

Harasymiw, Mark.
Chasing a tornado / by Mark Harasymiw.
    p. cm. — (Thrill seekers)
Includes index.
ISBN 978-1-4824-0139-4 (pbk.)
ISBN 978-1-4824-0141-7 (6-pack)
ISBN 978-1-4824-0138-7 (library binding)
1. Tornadoes — Juvenile literature. 2. Storms — Juvenile literature. 3. Meteorologists — Juvenile literature. I. Harasymiw, Mark. II. Title.
QC941.3 H24 2014
551.553—dc23

First Edition

Published in 2014 by
Gareth Stevens Publishing
111 East 14th Street, Suite 349
New York, NY 10003

Copyright © 2014 Gareth Stevens Publishing

Designer: Michael J. Flynn
Editor: Therese Shea

Photo credits: Cover, p. 1 (tornado) solarseven/Shutterstock.com; cover, p. 1 (van and storm chasers) Jeff Hutchens/Getty Images; p. 5 (tornado) AFP/Getty Images; p. 5 (inset) Brett Deering/Getty Images; pp. 7, 17, 27 Carsten Peter/National Geographic/Getty Images; p. 9 Tom Bean/Photographer's Choice/Getty Images; p. 10 Mike Theiss/National Geographic/Getty Images; pp. 11, 21 Minerva Studio/Shutterstock.com; pp. 13, 23 (inset), 25 Jim Reed/Photo Researchers/Getty Images; pp. 14, 26 courtesy of the National Oceanic and Atmospheric Administration; p. 15 Willoughby Owen/Flickr/Getty Images; p. 19 Ryan McGinnis/Flickr/Getty Images; p. 23 (main) Roger Wissmann/Shutterstock.com; p. 29 The Washington Post/Getty Images.

Printed in the United States of America

CPSIA compliance information: Batch #CW14GS: For further information contact Gareth Stevens, New York, New York at 1-800-542-2595.

CONTENTS

Words in the glossary appear in **bold** type
the first time they are used in the text.

ONE DEADLY HOUR

On May 20, 2013, a tornado touched down south of Oklahoma City, Oklahoma. In just over an hour, it traveled east about 17 miles (27 km) with winds blowing more than 200 miles (322 km) an hour. It tore up houses, schools, and hospitals in its path. By the time the tornado was done, more than 1,000 buildings were destroyed and nearly 1,200 were **damaged**.

One survivor recalled hearing the roar of the tornado as she waited in a shelter for it to pass. After it was gone, she walked out to see the damage, but there was "nothing there." Her neighborhood had been wiped out.

The Human Cost

Twenty-four people died because of the Oklahoma tornado on May 20, 2013, including 10 children. More than 375 were injured. Sadly, the same area experienced a similar tragedy in May 1999. In a little over an hour, that tornado killed 46, injured 800, and caused about $1.5 billion in damage.

The Oklahoma Insurance Department **estimated** the cost of rebuilding after the 2013 tornado would likely top $2 billion.

MOVING IN THE WRONG DIRECTION

While most people travel away from destructive weather events, a few move toward them. These people are called storm chasers. They chase for many reasons: Some are scientists. Others are news reporters. Photographers and filmmakers also follow storms. Some people are just very interested in weather!

Some only hunt tornadoes, making them tornado chasers. Tornado chasing may be the hardest "chasing" of all. That's because, unlike many hurricanes, blizzards, or other storms, tornadoes usually only last a few minutes. So, it takes a lot of work—and a good amount of luck—to be in the right place to spot a tornado.

More Threats

Blinding rains, huge pieces of hail, and frequent lightning strikes can all be parts of the storms that produce tornadoes. These make traveling to and observing tornadoes even more dangerous. No matter what their reason for pursuing tornadoes, chasers must realize that they're putting themselves in dangerous situations.

Besides the extreme danger of high-speed tornado winds, storm chasers face many other risks.

BORN FROM THUNDERSTORMS

A tornado occurs when weather opposites crash in just the right—or wrong—conditions. Most tornadoes form from large thunderstorms.

Scientists know a thunderstorm can arise when a warm **front** and a cold front meet or a wet air mass and a dry air mass run into each other. That's because when warm, wet air rises and cools, it **condenses** to make clouds. Cooler air rushes in to take the warm air's place. This change in pressure causes wind. The movement of air up into the atmosphere is called an updraft. The cold air traveling down is called a downdraft.

Extreme Thunderstorms

During an extreme thunderstorm, called a supercell, you can't see the spinning winds that may become a tornado until it's too late. If there were no dust or **debris** in the winds of a tornado, you wouldn't be able to see it, either.

Tornado chasers want to be there when a tornado comes out of a supercell—but not too close!

Though it's not easy to **predict** a tornado, like a thunderstorm, scientists understand the chain of events that lead to a tornado. First, there's a change in a storm's wind direction and speed. A very large updraft begins spinning. This mass of air, called the mesocyclone, is the birthplace of tornadoes—twisting funnels that touch the ground.

Most tornadoes touch down for only a few minutes, but they can last longer than an hour. Scientists aren't quite sure what makes a tornado stop. A large mass of cold air can cut off its supply of warm air. It's hard to know when this will happen.

The Mesocyclone

The mesocyclone can be 2 to 6 miles (3 to 10 km) wide. It hangs low in the sky and is easy to spot. There's a 50 percent chance a tornado can occur once a mesocyclone forms, often within just 30 minutes.

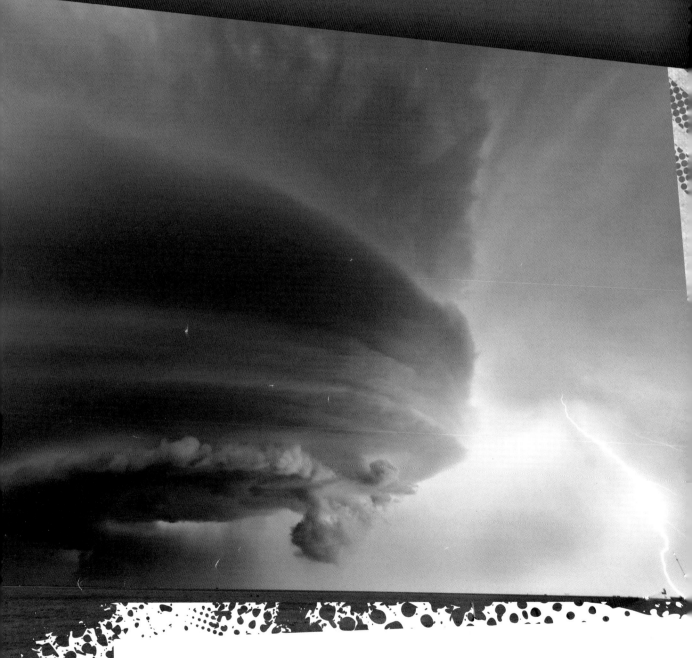

Mesocyclones may carry electrical charges that create lightning.

TRICKY TO TRACK

Just like weather scientists, or meteorologists, study weather **data** to provide people with forecasts, tornado chasers spend a lot of time examining weather to pinpoint the likely places that a tornado may form.

When they find the right conditions, tornado chasers might spend hours driving to the right spot. After getting there, the weather may have changed. Or the weather might be exactly right, but a tornado doesn't form. In that case, the tornado chasers have to get back into the car and try again at another time and another place. People are still unsure why some thunderstorms create tornadoes and some do not.

Moving Target

Even if tornado chasers are right about a tornado's appearance, there's another challenge to finding one. Tornadoes move—and sometimes fast. Most have an average speed of 30 miles (48 km) per hour, though some have been clocked at 70 miles (113 km) per hour! Most tornadoes travel southwest to northeast.

Much of tornado chasing is studying and traveling.

TORNADO ALLEY

Tornado chasers usually spend their time in an area in the central United States called Tornado Alley. This is where most tornadoes take place, from Texas north toward Canada. Moist air from the Gulf of Mexico mixes with dry air from New Mexico and Arizona. April, May, June, and July are the most likely months for tornadoes to occur here.

However, tornadoes can happen anytime and anywhere if conditions are right. In fact, they have happened in every US state and on every continent except Antarctica. The United States experiences the most tornadoes, though.

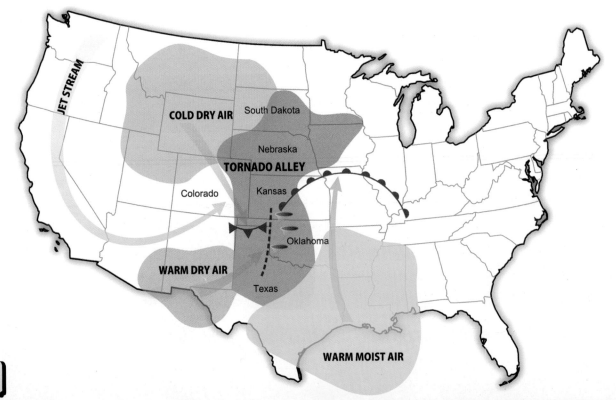

The map on page 14 shows all the weather conditions that may affect and create a tornado such as the one below.

Watches and Warnings

Do you know the difference between a tornado watch and a tornado warning? A watch means a tornado is possible. It's a good idea to keep an eye on the weather. A warning means a tornado has been spotted or that a thunderstorm looks likely to create one. People should seek shelter quickly.

CHASING EQUIPMENT

Tornado chasers carry a wide range of equipment to help them locate and examine a tornado. Cameras help a chaser record the behavior of tornadoes, and computers can be used to provide up-to-date weather maps as well as send findings to the Internet. Radios and walkie-talkies keep a team of chasers in contact with each other.

Chasers also pack more advanced equipment such as radiosondes. Radiosondes are weather balloons that measure temperature, air pressure, and wind speed and direction. Some chasers even have their own **radar** to track the tornado, just like you've seen on the news.

Tornado Technology of the Future?

Students at Oklahoma State University have **designed** drones, aircraft controlled from the ground, that could someday provide a deeper understanding of tornadoes and how they form. SPAVs (Storm Penetrating Air Vehicles) are small but could carry containers of **sensors**, called dropsondes, into storms.

You can see the equipment loaded onto the roof of this chaser's truck. If a tornado gets too close, this gear will likely be torn off by winds and debris.

THE TIV-2

Filmmaker Sean Casey built an amazing truck for tornado chasing that he calls the TIV-2. TIV stands for "Tornado Intercept Vehicle." The TIV-2 is covered in steel 1/8 inch (3.2 mm) thick and special hardened glass to protect the people and equipment inside. It even has an armored **turret** that can completely spin around so that the IMAX camera inside can record tornadoes in any direction.

With all these parts, the TIV-2 is heavy. It weighs about 14,000 pounds (6,350 kg). Despite its weight, it has a top speed of 100 miles (161 km) per hour and can travel off road!

Not Easily Picked Up

The TIV-2 has panels that lower to the ground. This makes it less likely that tornado winds can get under the vehicle and pick it up or blow it over. It even has spikes that drive into the ground to further strengthen its grip on the earth.

Sean Casey has plans to improve his amazing vehicle.
Watch out for the TIV-3!

CLASSIFYING TORNADOES

Though tornado chasers have made tools and vehicles that can stand up to some tornado conditions, it's not always possible for them to get to a tornado in order to measure its strength. So, tornadoes are **classified** according to how much damage they've done using the Enhanced Fujita (EF) Scale.

The EF Scale has six different ratings: EF0 through EF5. The higher the EF number, the more destructive the tornado is. By examining the damage to different kinds of objects—such as houses, apartment buildings, and trees—scientists are able to estimate the wind speed of a tornado.

The First Fujita Scale

The Enhanced Fujita Scale was first used in 2007. It was based on the Fujita Scale designed by Dr. Ted Fujita of the University of Chicago in 1971. The original Fujita Scale was replaced because many believed it overestimated wind speeds. Even though the EF Scale is an improvement, it still provides only an estimate of a tornado's wind speed.

Most tornadoes are rated EF0 or EF1. Most deaths occur during EF4 and EF5 tornadoes.

OPERATIONAL EF SCALE

EF Number	3-Second Gust (mph)
0	65–85
1	86–110
2	111–135
3	136–165
4	166–200
5	Over 200

FAMOUS CHASERS

One of the first pioneers of storm chasing was Roger Jensen. Jensen was born in North Dakota in 1933 and very early in life became interested in storms. In the 1950s, he began photographing and chasing storms with his father. His name became well known, and his photos were published in many newsletters and magazines.

Another important person in tornado chasing is David Hoadley. He began chasing storms in 1956. He was astounded at the damage they could do. In 1977, Hoadley started a national newsletter called "Storm Track." He wanted storm chasers to have a place to share experiences, views, and camera tips and tricks. *Storm Track* is now a magazine.

Tornado Maker

Neil Ward was one of the first tornado chasers who was also a scientist. He worked at the National Severe Storms Laboratory (NSSL) in Oklahoma. Ward was able to use his scientific background as well as his observations of storms to make minitornadoes in his laboratory!

In one of the storms Roger Jensen was chasing, he photographed hailstones larger than baseballs, like this one.

Tim Samaras was a researcher and tornado chaser for more than 35 years. His goal was to learn why some storms create tornadoes while others don't. He hoped this knowledge could increase the warning time for a tornado so that people could get to safety. Samaras reported the current warning time is only about 17 minutes. "Wouldn't it be great if that lead time could be 30 minutes?" he asked.

Sadly, Samaras and his team—his son Paul and storm chaser Carl Young—died in a tornado near El Reno, Oklahoma, in May 2013. Hopefully, in the future, we'll know enough about tornadoes so there's less need for chasers to put their lives in danger.

What Does a Tornado Feel Like?

Tim Samaras designed a special tool called a probe that can be placed in a tornado's path. It gathers information such as temperature, pressure, and moisture on the ground. It measured the drop in air pressure in an EF5 tornado. The drop was "like stepping into an elevator and hurtling up 1,000 feet (305 m) in 10 seconds."

Tim Samaras was inspired to become a tornado chaser by the movie *The Wizard of Oz.*

THE NSSL

The NSSL is a national research laboratory under the National Oceanic and Atmospheric Administration (NOAA). Located in Norman, Oklahoma, the NSSL works with the University of Oklahoma and state governments to improve weather forecasts.

One of the famous tools that the NSSL created was TOTO. TOTO stands for TOtable Tornado Observatory. It was a barrel filled with scientific equipment that was built to be carried by a tornado. Unfortunately, TOTO wasn't much of a success because of tornadoes' unpredictable nature. However, it did provide valuable information about storms and mesocyclones. New kinds of weather balloons, radar systems, and probes have proven more helpful to the NSSL in recent years.

At the NSSL, sometimes storm chasing is a part of the job.

Tornado Spotters

Some people are storm "spotters." They don't travel around like chasers. Instead, they work from where they live. They report to organizations such as the National Weather Service about local severe weather conditions as they happen. Spotters are trained to collect needed information.

27

STORM SMARTS

Some people don't understand the unpredictable nature of tornadoes. They stay outside or pull over in their cars so they can take pictures or video of the approaching weather. Sadly, some of these people are struck by lightning when the storm is over a mile away. Others are hit by debris carried a great distance by wind. Still others don't realize just how fast the tornado is moving.

Each year, people are injured or even lose their lives because they don't realize the true danger of tornadoes. Many tornado chasers, like Tim Samaras, put their lives on the line to save others. People should respect that by being smart in severe weather.

Don't Be an Amateur

Amateur storm and tornado chasers—those who just want to see the storm in action for no research or public safety purpose—put themselves and others in danger. They may need to be rescued if they get in trouble. Their cars can clog up roads and keep emergency vehicles from helping others.

Many people's lives are saved by storm shelters like this one.

GLOSSARY

amateur: someone who does something without much experience or skill

classify: to assign something to a category or class based on shared qualities

condense: to lose heat and change from a gas into a liquid

damage: harm. Also, to cause harm.

data: facts and figures

debris: the remains of something that has been broken

design: to create the pattern or shape of something

estimate: to make a careful guess about an answer based on the known facts

front: the border between two masses of air

predict: to guess what will happen in the future based on facts or knowledge

radar: a machine that uses radio waves to locate and identify objects

sensor: a tool that can detect changes in its surroundings

turret: an armored structure on top of a vehicle that can be moved side to side or in a circle

FOR MORE INFORMATION

BOOKS

Jeffrey, Gary. *Hurricane Hunters & Tornado Chasers.* New York, NY: Rosen Central, 2008.

Rebman, Renée. *How Do Tornadoes Form?* New York, NY: Marshall Cavendish Benchmark, 2011.

Scavuzzo, Wendy. *Tornado Alert!* New York, NY: Crabtree Publishing, 2011.

WEBSITES

How Tornadoes Work
www.howstuffworks.com/nature/climate-weather/storms/tornado.htm
Read step by step how tornadoes emerge from thunderstorms.

Severe Weather 101
www.nssl.noaa.gov/education/svrwx101/
Find answers to questions about many different kinds of terrible weather conditions, including tornadoes.

INDEX